Somewhere During the Spin Cycle

Somewhere During the Spin Cycle

Poems

Joseph Mills

Press 53
Winston-Salem, North Carolina

Press 53
PO Box 30314
Winston-Salem, NC 27130

First Edition

Cover design by Kevin Watson
Cover art by Liliana Italiano

Cover art "Sudestada," by Liliana Italiano used by permission of the artist.

Printed in the United States of America

ISBN 0-9772283-6-3

Acknowledgments

Thanks to the editors of the following publications where these poems (or earlier versions) first appeared:

Amelia: "Somewhere During the Spin Cycle"
a-pos-tro-phe: "Speech After Long Silence," "After Another Late Dinner Alone" and "Souvenir"
Artful Mind: "Recipes"
Blue Mesa Review: "11:00, Friday Night," "Last Call," "Rabat" and "Visions"
Coe Review: "Where the Locals Go" and "As If Motion Were Action"
Coracle: "La Fête de la Musique: Locquenolé"
CQ: "The Moment"
Domicile: "The Only Photograph I Have of My Father," "In the Night," "Backroads," "Heaven's Gate," "Portrait" and "Aisle Twelve"
Enopoetica: "Twenty Years Later I Make a Realization About Her Shampoo" and "Moonrise Bay Winery"
Foliate Oak: "A Snowy Evening in Iowa" and "The Optometrist Explains How We Carry the Dead Within Us"
Haight Ashbury Literary Journal: "Practicing"
Kinesis: "Purgatory"
Latitude Magazine: "Twenty Years Later I Make a Realization About Her Shampoo"
New Writing: " Sympathy"
North Carolina Literary Review: "Aging"
Main Street Rag: "Introductions Made Easy"
MountainRise: "Turning in Grades" and "When My Students Ask Why They Need Poetry"
Oxygen: "On Finally Learning to Bake in My Thirties"
Poetry Bone: "Storm: early morning"
Portland Review: "Talking to a Miner in the Columbine Cafe about the Memory of Bone"
Rockford Review: " The Indiana State Waterski Championship"
Santa Clara Review: "Bordeaux 1995," "Max" and "Beaujolais"
Southcoast Poetry Journal: "After A Month"
Timber Creek Review: "Shooting a Scene in the Parkview Cemetery"

To my father, Robert E. Mills,

who taught me how to drive,
who bought me my first bus ticket,
train ticket, and plane ticket, and
who showed me that I should never
be afraid to pack up and go.

Contents

Somewhere During the Spin Cycle 13

The Only Photograph I Have of My Father 14

The Indiana State Waterski Championship 15

Blowing Up Barbie 16

Talking to a Miner in the Columbine Cafe
about the Memory of Bone 17

Where the Locals Go 18

Conversations on the North Rim 19

A Snowy Evening in Iowa 20

As If Motion Was Action 21

Portrait 27

American Beaujolais 28

Bordeaux 1995 30

Introductions Made Easy 31

La Fête de la Musique: Locquenolé 32

Purgatory 33

Rabat 34

Gibraltar 1987 35

Souvenir 36

Practicing 38

How to Search for a Poem to Read at a
Wedding 40

Aisle Twelve 42

God's Acre, North Carolina, Where They
Bury the Sexes Separately 44

Aging 46

In the Night 47

Glimpses 48

Night After Night 49

The Moment 50

Storm: early morning   51
After a Month   52
On Finally Learning to Bake in My Thirties   53
Recipes   54
Twenty Years Later I Make a Realization
        About Her Shampoo   56
Moonrise Bay Winery   57
Service   58
Speech After Long Silence   59
The Optometrist Explains How We Carry
        the Dead Within Us   60
After Another Late Dinner Alone   62
Shooting a Scene in the Parkview Cemetery   63
11:00, Friday Night   73
Visions   74
Between Diving and Surfacing   76
When My Students Ask Why They Need
        Poetry   77
Max   78
Turning in Grades   80
Sympathy   81
Poetry Lesson   82
Heaven's Gate   83
Last Call   84

Somewhere During the Spin Cycle

Somewhere During the Spin Cycle

Maybe it's the ball player being interviewed
on the TV bolted above the dryers
or the two kids playing and punching
the video machine
or the late night October wind,
but there's your brother,
drunk and crying,
running through the woods
behind your house,
his unclipped duffel
spilling clothes behind him,
and your father
sitting in the kitchen,
shirtless, gaunt,
his clenched face
watching
as we search for a flashlight
to follow the trail
of socks and t-shirts
back to the overgrown diamond
where Ted is passed out
in deep right field
and we sit between second and third,
smoking the pack of Marlboros
your sister bought for us,
folding clothes,
and talking about where we will go
when we're his age.

The Only Photograph I Have of My Father

In 1958, a young man stands
in half unzipped coveralls.
A white t-shirt shows underneath.
He has thick black hair cut in a flattop.
He holds a wrench in his right hand.
A plain brick building is behind him.
The sky is a winter grey.

Each time I sit at my desk,
this smiling mechanic,
the age of my students,
looks past my shoulder
at someone holding a Kodak Instamatic
who is calling his name.
I recognize the posture;
he's trying to be patient,
but he needs to go back inside
to finish a transmission job,
and then there is something else to do.
There is always something else to do.

Dad, before you go
just once
look over here.

The Indiana State Water Ski Championship

When Tommy miscalculated
and crunched the jump
so hard he slid off the side
and his skis spun his body
headfirst into the water,
Billy's mother ran out
from behind a tree
moaning,
I'm sorry. I'm sorry.
as if she feared
one gloved hand
of his floating corpse
would point towards her,
and when she saw him
crawl into the tow boat,
shaken, but okay,
she looked around, annoyed
at having revealed herself,
as if at every tournament
we didn't notice her
crouching on the shore
one hand covering her eyes
one hand carving hexes,
muttering incantations
against all the children
who weren't her son.

Blowing up Barbie

We must have started with army men,
tanks, and military trucks.
We'd bury firecrackers
in the carefully graded dirt,
then light them
blowing the green pieces off balance.
There probably was a matchbox car
or Tonka truck stage,
but eventually we moved on
to the civilians,
Barbie, Ken, and Skipper
characters from a world
of showpiece accessories and tea sets,
and soon we were roleplaying as well

I'm just going to run an errand...

Isn't it lovely out today...

So then I said to her...

imagining their perkiness
right before the earth beneath their feet
shattered.
It discolored their skin
ruined their carefully matched wardrobes
but never dismembered them.
Since they were always dazed
but ambulatory,
it was irritating
that our sister cried so much.

Talking to a Miner in the Columbine Cafe
about the Memory of Bone

He says what bothers him most
is having to wear the watch on his right.
He keeps trying his left,
cinching the leather
strap deep into the skin
but it keeps slipping off

and when it does
he says he can feel
the watch slide towards his hand
and he curls his fingers
to catch it and he's stunned
when it hits the ground.

Where the Locals Go

A mile from the parking lot
a dead oak
hollowed by fire
marks where
a faint path
leaves the main trail
into the thicket.

It goes
to a bend in the river
where there's no rope swing,
no large rocks,
no old fishing hole.

The bank is steep,
covered with thistles,
and it's almost impossible
to keep your footing,
but if you wade into the water
far enough to anchor yourself
on the submerged sandbar,
you can lean upstream
hold yourself
like a dancer in mid-leap
for minutes
hours
until night falls
and you're still balanced
on one foot
a black liquid rope
braiding around you
the moon in your face.

Conversations on the North Rim

Squatting near the edge,
your back to the miles-wide absence
that four million people photograph each year,
you call me over,
point inside a cracked fist of rock
say,
look,
I think it's some kind of beetle.

Some night
when there's no moon
and no stars
you say you want to stand
at the rim
and hold out your arms
I won't be able to see anything
but it will be there.

We loop our way
through the Kaibab evening
back to our campsite.
Music comes from somewhere
and you stop to listen.
That's Jaco on bass,
you say
closing your eyes
and tilting your head.

As constellations circle above
and the Colorado river cuts deeper,
I watch the skin tighten across your throat.

A Snowy Evening in Iowa

Afterwards, I slept so soundly
I didn't hear her get up
to cook the steaks,
potatoes and gravy,
green beans and onions,
or set the table
with candles,
and later by the hearth,
as we drank Irish cream,
she adjusted the comforter
her grandmother had made
and casually mentioned
the coffee in the freezer,
the need to set the alarm,
the weather forecast,
those jews who owned
her company and the country.

I said nothing,
then left in the morning
and never called
like a diner who eats
a bad meal without complaining
but doesn't come back.
I didn't realize until years later
how politeness and silence
can be a form of cowardice,
and how she had a right
to know why I fled
my glimpse of that life
that warm comfortable cocoon
between fire and ice
where all the dishes match.

As if Motion Was Action

i.

My friend's sister drove from Detroit
to Portland, Oregon
and never stopped for gas,
never even touched the accelerator.
She says she sat cross-legged and
The Lord filled my tank.

Maybe that's why
I always wait so long
before stopping,
deliberately descending
far below Empty,
giving the Lord a chance.

ii.

Drive long enough
and mile markers skitter
across the road
like rabid shadows,
the "winding curves"
snake
from their signs,
the pavement itself
shrugs, stretches, twists
until you're convinced
you're riding
the back of a living thing.

Doing a straight shot
from Salt Lake City to Chicago,
I stopped after eighteen hours
at a rest area in Iowa
just long enough
to take care of business
and refuse a ride
to a hitchhiker,
but at the Illinois line
I realized
he had secretly climbed
into the backseat,
so steering with my knees
I struck out wildly behind me
screaming, *Get out,
goddamnit, get out.*

iii.

After the Trinity test,
Enrico Fermi found himself
unable to drive home.
It seemed as if
"the car were jumping
from curve to curve
skipping the straight stretches
in between."

iv.

Drive long enough
and the trip becomes
nothing,
an absence;
for all the miles
that became hours
that became simply
driving
there's nothing
that you can remember
no landscape, no exits, no stops.
At one point perhaps
there was a sun
and then at some point
there wasn't.

v.

In the museum,
I saw Kerouac's manuscript;
the dirty yellow teletype
neatly spooled and displayed.
The plaque explained
how he had written to Cassidy,
saying that it looked like a road
when rolled out in his living room,
and in the next case
was Kerouac himself
on the Steve Allen show
reading the book's ending
every five minutes,
each time looking as tense
and out of place
as the time before,
and if the VCR were stopped,
the cassette broken open,
the tape unspooled
across the museum floor,
maybe it too
would look like a road.

Maybe.

vi.

One is figure.
One is ground.
The stops become the spaces
between the moving
the apartments the stops
between the traveling
as if what you want
is always only a little farther.
This is the legacy
of Columbus
that first American traveler
who wrote in his diaries
about all those helpful tribes
advising him
it isn't here
what you want
is further along
keep going
keep going.

Portrait

At lunch, Grams tells me of her grandfather's brother, the one with the cocked eye, who moved to a Methodist neighborhood and how they put a noose around his neck to scare him away and how he went crazy but his family refused to leave. She tells me about getting married at nineteen to escape her mother and how her husband who had three Studebakers when she met him jumped from a window six years later during the Depression, thinking his insurance policy would take care of her and the children. She describes the tornado that swept through her town when she was young, how many cups of coffee you can get from a pound, a trip to California during the War to see her sons on furlough, the first time she tasted champagne, the Russian churches of Sitka, Alaska where my father took her a few years ago, and the way her niece holds a fork. She says her younger sister, who at eighty-seven is bedridden, has given up. She shakes her head and stops eating. I ask her if she wants more crackers for her soup. Am I having some? she wants to know. Whatever I have is fine with her. She asks if I go to church. I tell her I do then on Sundays I go to the library. After we eat, she'll feel her way along the unfamiliar hallway to her room where she'll nap. Upon waking, she'll re-make her bed and dust the dresser again. She must push herself she says. That's what we live for.

American Beaujolais

When it arrived
I was in a Vegas coffeeshop
trying not to listen
to the next table
the loud woman in sunglasses
the loud man with thick fingers

why can't I
for once
why not

He orders the waitress
to take back her food
although she insists

It's okay. Stop it.
It's fine. Damnit.

but even they quiet
when the pompadoured waiter
begins a solemn weave
around his tables
the new currency
displayed
between his hands

It's the hundred, see?
Have you seen it?
See?

explaining to the family from Jersey
the markings, the differences,
as they pass it around,
like a baby photo,
oohing and ahing,

then in 17 weeks
the fifties
then in 17 weeks
the twenties
then in 17 weeks

a bus boy asks
if he can show the guys
in the kitchen

Okay, but be careful
and bring it back.
Bring it back soon.

Bordeaux 1995

In a two bedroom apartment
crammed with people, smoke,
a dozen wine bottles,
a woman from Galway
shoulders her way through a jig
with a woman from Belfast.
Claire turns 22 tomorrow,
and tonight with her brown hair
tucked under her new hat,
something in the curve of her cheek
reminds me
of hiking with my brother
on Mt. Tamalpais
and talking about God,
Smokey the Bear,
little league baseball,
as we lay under redwoods,
looking at the stars
spread across the sky
like freckles on an Irish girl.

Introductions Made Easy

If only people wore labels,
their foreheads clearly displaying
their appelation, varietal,
alcohol content,
think of the time it would save.
We could cut out the small talk,
the "where are you from?"
and "what do you do?"
Appropriate pairings
would be more obvious,
we would know if they met
government standards,
and we would have a better idea
who might improve with age
and who we should enjoy now.

La Fête de la Musique: Locquenolé

No matter what the bands play
rock and roll, salsa, folk,
the people from the home
move the same way,
each locked into a rhythm
and continuing it
even during the set breaks.
A tall blonde steps forward
rocks back, steps forward
rocks back. A woman in green
keeps her feet planted
and swings her arms and hips
left, right,
        left, right
as steady as a metronome.
Another waltzes in a circle
that expands to enclose
the entire plaza.

At 3 a.m. as the last band
does a Chuck Berry medley,
they try to come together,
joining hands and elbows,
swaying as a group,
but each is unable
or unwilling to give
up their particular motions
and one refuses
to join at all,
shaking his head violently
as he spins
around his housemates
staying just outside
their yearning fingers.

Purgatory

I used to imagine purgatory
as a combination dry cleaner/car wash,
our souls hung on hangers,
like sides of beef on hooks,
cycling through a wash
of fire
burning cleaner and cleaner
each time through
until we arrived
at a sunlit parking lot
and were burnished by angels,

but perhaps it is this
circling through the fog
under a "fasten seatbelts" sign
and a voice every thirty minutes
saying it will be
just a little longer
before we can land in the city
where you are asleep
between clean white sheets
arms cradling
an extra pillow.

Rabat

The women henna their hands
weaving rust-colored lines
into tattoos of celebration
across their brown skin.
If you follow one
of these intricate designs
you can trace a life
along veins of joy
and sorrow so deep
into the flesh
that you begin
to hope she will
fold each finger
and lock you
safe inside
her fist.

Gibraltar 1987

After a month in Morocco
where people stare
at our blonde hair and skin,
it's soothing to be back
in a culture so close
to our own.
It's like a little Britain, I say
delighted with the pubs,
the fish and chips, the people
who speak like John Cleese,
and in the morning,
at the cafe next to our hotel,
an Irish man drinking tea
is shot in the head.

Souvenir

At the American Deli in London
just down the hill from St. Paul's
where we're trying to dry off
because the King's Arms across the street
doesn't serve coffee
a woman pulling a grocery cart
with a small white dog
tethered to the bottom rack
stops beside the door.
After pushing the animal
against the shelter of the wall
she enters
moves towards the counter
stopping every few feet
to look back.

A teenager in a redwhiteandblue paper hat
yells with a Cockney accent
Oy! I just mopped there.

At the counter the woman pulls
change from her coat pockets
without speaking
the counterman pushes
two burgers forward.
She puts these in her coat
hesitates as if she wants
to ask or order something
then turns away.
Outside she tries to get her cart
across the rain-slick street

but it slides into the flooded gutter
pulling the dog with it.
You go to help her cross
and when safely on the other side
she reaches into her bags
and gives you a small potted plant.
Long after we're warm again
we sit and look
at the mottled leaves
the green plastic container
neither willing
to point out
there's no place
for it in our luggage.

Practicing

You forget how many bad ways there are to live
until you're driving around the addresses
you circled in the classifieds
looking at the barbed-wire,
the peeling paint,
the buildings tucked under freeways
or next to parking garages.

Inside, you wander the rooms,
reminding yourself
each appears larger
when it's empty.
You try to picture
your furniture arranged
somehow on the brown carpets,
your photos on the off-white walls,
your dishes in the sink.

Where will you put your books?
The phone? The garbage?
And the nearest grocery?
The gas station? What
will life be like? That's what
you really want to ask
the person waiting at the door.
And when you find yourself saying
maybe it wouldn't
be so bad
for a while,

you know you have to look
at yet another place
or wait for tomorrow's paper
or maybe you'll come back later
drive up slowly
pretending you're coming home
pretending this is who you are.

How to Search for a Poem to
Read at a Wedding

Go to the obvious places: Shakespeare's sonnets,
anthologies of love poems.
Disdain what you find there as too obvious.
Pull *Bartlett's Quotations* from the shelf.
Scan the entries on marriage:
a necessary evil, a noose, a dirge, a cage, slavery.
Decide these might not be appropriate.
Pour over the dozens of poetry books
you've acquired through the years.
Search through bookstores.
Surf the Internet.
In desperation, enter a Hallmark store.
Discover nothing that seems right.

Begin to consider not going.
Ask yourself what would happen
if you were sick—
people get sick after all.
If you don't read a poem,
they will still get married.
Why travel hundreds of miles
and spend hundreds of dollars?
If you don't go,
they will still get married.
Feel ashamed.

Begin again.

Realize what's been missing from the poems,
how none of them describe
the first time you saw Martha,

how she was standing in the doorway
of a Vietnamese restaurant, waiting
for Russ and you to arrive after work
and as you walked up the street in the rain
Russ said, *Watch this. I can make my sweetie wave.*
Russ waved.
Martha waved back.
He said, *Watch. I can make her do it again.*
He waved.
She waved back.
He said, *Watch this...*
and at each step
they waved and smiled
delighted to be playing in the rain
to be seeing one another
after a whole day's separation,
knowing in a few moments
they would be warm and dry
side by side.

A celebration and witness of this,
this joyful closing of distance,
this sense of watching someone you love come home,
this is what you're looking for.

Aisle Twelve

They're in their eighties
or seventies
or anyway have reached the age
where time has molded their spines
into that wire hanger curve.
The woman has her hands hooked
onto the shopping cart;
the man hangs on her elbow,
and they slowly tack
along the vegetables,
two boats tied together.
I don't know why I linger,
pretending to decide
between diced and crushed tomatoes.
Perhaps I'm searching for clues
as to what we'll be like.
As they float past,
he says, *you wanted plums,*
and she responds,
you need Sanka too.
He puts his hand on her back
to reassure or push off,
says, *I'll meet you*
at that one cashier,
then moves away,
and this simple separation,
this confident casting off,
astounds me.
I want to follow both,

assure myself that yes
all will go smoothly
for them,
for us,
but I turn to my list,
continue to search
for those things
we decided this morning we need:
deodorant, shampoo,
my coffee, your fruit.

God's Acre, North Carolina, Where
They Bury the Sexes Separately

My grandmother suffered, died, and was buried on the left side of a dual plot in Parkview, Illinois. My grandfather said that he wasn't surprised she went first. She was always packed before him, and for forty years he had relied on her to warm up the bed. He said he would probably join her soon, and, just as he used to turn off the lights and lock the doors each night after she had climbed the stairs, he prepared for the end of his life, selling the house, checking into an assisted living complex, and paying his funeral bills in advance. Might as well face the inevitable, he said.

We prepared ourselves as well, thinking about what we might say at the funeral and how we might feel, practicing our mourning, wanting to be ready.

Finally, the phone did ring, and it was the director from the home. My mother listened, then put the phone down and turned to my father. *It's Dad*, she said, and even as I braced myself as if we were about to be in a car wreck, part of me admired how stunned my mother looked.

He's married Mrs. Brooks.

We knew her. She lived down the hall and sometimes joined us for lunch when we visited. She was a nice lady, but what about the inevitable?

And what would happen later? Where would they each go? Would Mrs. Brooks join Mr. Brooks? Did they have a dual plot somewhere? Or was this musical chairs and you went down where you were when the music stopped? Could we put an addition on in Parkview and wedge grandpa in between his two women? Would the three of them then approach St. Peter arm in arm in arm? My mother insisted seniority should rule as if Grandma had clocked in years of service that should count for something. My father felt cremation offered Solomon-like possibilities, especially if the inevitable came to Mrs. Brooks first and Grandpa married again. And again.

Oh to be Moravian and at judgment day simply line up, boys on the right, girls on the left, alone together, smiling and waving at all the ones you loved.

Aging

To speak of a wine's future
is to speak of our own desires.
How we hope as we age
that we'll become more
harmonous, less acidic,
that our tannins will mellow.
We recognize that right now
we have a burst of flavor,
an energy, a liveliness,
but also a harshness
which later may soften
until we're more balanced,
more approachable,
easier to appreciate.
Hold onto us
we believe
we'll get better.

In the Night

Two stories below,
the furnace sputters on
straining to warm
this poorly insulated house,
and I wonder
if it will last
another winter
and how much longer
we can put off
replacing the dishwasher,
the roof, the hot water boiler,
the car we bought new
only ten years ago.

As I count my worries
like sheep
you roll toward me,
push a leg over my hip,
murmur into my back,
It's all too short, isn't it?
then fall back asleep
before hearing me whisper,
yes.
yes.

Glimpses

Sometimes when I'm dragging
the garbage to the curb
or walking the dog,
I'll glimpse the moon,
through the trees
or over a roof
and be so startled,
I'll stop to gawk.
At forty
I should be used
to such a sight,
yet each time
I feel the urge
to find someone
and say, *Look! The Moon!*
Isn't it amazing?

And ten years after
the first glimpse I had
of you talking
on the phone,
I'll be thinking about
the laundry,
the grocery,
the next obligation,
and I will suddenly see
you coming to the door
or pulling into our drive,
and I'll find myself
amazed
stunned still
by the pull of your presence.

Night After Night

I'm surprised you would sleep with such a man,
someone who takes his clothes off in the dark
to hide his gray and gut, who slides beneath
the sheets as quick as his stiff back allows,
someone older than your father was when
we first met. Did it happen so slowly,
hair by hair, you didn't notice for years
the man I had become? But now you must.
The dark no longer hides my belly sag
or aging breath. If you felt tricked, betrayed,
I'd understand. And yet each night your hands
reach out to pull me close. Who wouldn't be
surprised by this soft clasp? It makes me change
I'm sorry to *Good night, my love, good night.*

The Moment

You think when the plane falls
in those few minutes
you'll turn to your lover
and say

It was a good life.
Thank you.
I loved you, I love you.

but the moment comes
hitting black ice on the highway
and as the car spins
at 80 miles an hour
you turn to me
grab my arm
say

Oh shit. Shit.
I'm sorry, I'm sorry,
I'm sorry.

Storm: early morning

she doesn't know what wakes her
she is asleep   then not asleep
walking through the house naked
hands reaching out
she doesn't know her eyes are open
until the kitchen
where the microwave blinks :12:00:

she feels through the dishes in the sink
finds the glass she used earlier
eases open the tap
lets the water rise

past the spot marked by her thumb
over the rim   across her wrist
off her elbow   to her hip
thigh
ankle
until she's again standing
in a floodtide

After A Month

I walk with outspread hands,
touching banisters,
tables, fresh candles,
burying my fingers in jars of flour,
but find nothing
like your skin
smooth as beachstone
or old driftwood
half buried in sand
covered by high tides,
the color of daylight moons.

On Finally Learning to Bake
in My Thirties

Is this where my mother's anger went?
Punched into flour and salt?
Hammering and pulling it into shape?

She always let the dough double-rise
perhaps because once
wasn't nearly enough
to turn that rage
into bread
light enough
to swallow.

Recipes

On Sunday, he cooks for the week,
shopping in the morning
and spending the afternoons
listening to the Oldies station,
chopping vegetables, frying chickens,
baking casseroles,
until the kitchen is filled with steam
and condensation thickens each wall,
so that when he steps onto the back porch
to lower another finished dish
into the freezer
the air seems cool, even chilly,
and as the heavy lid closes,
forming a seal,
for a moment,
he feels safe.

Sometimes, he still forgets
to cut the recipes in half,
and he stacks "her" portions
in the back corners.
If she returns,
she can excavate there
determine from his diet what he felt,
and perhaps she'll recognize
in those rising layers
of meals, those weekly cycles
of emotions getting smaller

and simpler,
how he tried to train himself
to forget her,
but how something
always remained,
prepared and frozen,
waiting to be eaten.

Twenty Years Later I Make a Realization About Her Shampoo

What do you smell, the winemaker asks,
and I hesistate to answer
because it's an old girlfriend
and weekends in her studio apartment,
milk carton bookshelves
and cracked walls and ceilings
whose stains we pretended formed maps
of countries like Mythica and Fornucopia.

He waits politely,
but you can't say
you smell a lover,
broken plaster,
old jokes,
a life you used to have.

Finally, he suggests,
Grapefruit?
and I realize yes,
that's it,
the nape of her neck,
her ears,
her hair.
Grapefruit.

Moonrise Bay Winery

After years of planning, planting, pruning,
tending first the idea and then the vines,
after the fingers blistered than calloused,
after evenings when you were too tired
to eat, after nights when you couldn't stop
calculating the costs in terms of tons,
vines, bottles, acres, all that you've denied
your daughters, finally the grapes are ripe.
You walk the green rows, pulling off clusters
of fruit until juice covers your arms
attracting clouds of butterflies. Here is
your harvest: these clapping wings of color,
these sweet handfuls of temporary grace.

Service

Wednesday is chicken night at the Legion. An all-you-can-eat buffet and fifty cent drafts. My father hates to miss it, and, when I'm in town, I go because there are so few things I can give him anymore. While we wait for a table, he talks with the other regulars and I drift around the lobby, looking at the familiar plaques and photographs. I always end up at the Last Man Rosters, the lists of names with gold stars indicating who has died. It's a lottery in reverse with fate pulling out tickets until only one remains. In the last few years, the World War II roster has become a constellation of loss. *A thousand a day are dying* someone says one night. *I heard it was two,* another says. A third notes, *Arlington is so full they'll have to close it soon.* The lobby quiets as everyone mentally reviews their arrangements. Then, I hear my father mock whisper, *I'll probably be put in a can and left on the curb.* He served in Korea, and there's a monument in Washington now, but they don't have a Last Man List. It annoys him—another way they've been uncounted—but I'm glad not to see his name waiting for its star. Finally, we're seated. I order a salad instead of the special, and my father looks away as if embarassed others will overhear. I clearly don't belong. Or maybe he's upset that he can't brag about *getting me in* when I'm not there to eat. We sit, surrounded by hungry veterans who served in Europe, the Pacific, Korea, Vietnam, the Gulf. This is their reward for living when they did, going where they were told, and still being around. Cheap beer, piles of legs and breasts and wings, and family sitting across a table as wide as a battlefield.

Speech After Long Silence

She says *listen*
swings her knee
and smiles at the pop.

It used to only happen in dreams.
Now I can do it
whenever I want.

She recocks her leg
makes it snap again
like gum.

This is my body now
she says
cracking it
repeatedly
fascinated by the sound
of her own dissolution.

The Optometrist Explains How We Carry The Dead Within Us

The doctor calls them floaters
these snips of thread
that move into my vision
if I focus
on nothing.

They're dead cells.
Harmless.
Everyone has them,
he says,
but let me know
if they increase.
It may be a sign
something's wrong.

He hands me a pamphlet
which explains in simple
reassuring terms
how your body
deteriorates;
The eye erodes,
crumbles;
pieces break off
and float across the pupils
showing you
your own dissolution.
The doctor compares them to breathing
something always there unnoticed
unless you concentrate
but they're more like

memories
affecting your vision
in ways you're usually not aware,
harmless
unless they increase
to the point
you can no longer see.

After Another Late Dinner Alone

Last night on the Underground
you stood before me
again
amused
wearing the tweed jacket
you had in college.
I was puzzled
by how solidly you stood
as the train rocked
until I noticed
curled around a post
anchoring you
was the long prehensile tail
you always joked about wanting.
I waited for you to speak or gesture
but only the tip of the tail moved
flexing like a finger.
When my stop came
I wanted to keep riding
to see where you were going.
I wanted you to explain
to tell me what I should have done
what I should do
all you must know now.
Instead, I stepped past
climbed the stairs to the surface
walked back to my temporary room.

Shooting a Scene in the Parkview Cemetery

i.

The director's annoyed
that we didn't get the shot
before the 10:30 burial,
so now we have to stop
for the *genuine* mourners
and by the time they're done
we'll have to reset
because of the different light.

As we eat Krispy Kremes
among the headstones,
some check their equipment,
others rehearse lines,
and one principal seems to sleep.

I watch the black crowd gather,
consider swelling the scene,
a comfort to family,
a puzzle to friends,
a stranger on the periphery,
marking the radius of grief.

ii.

In the caretaker's shed
where we dress,
bronze plates cover the walls.
Already engraved,
they announce the dead-to-be.

      Loving Husband
    May 15, 1932 -

        Veteran
       March 2, 1923 -

          Devoted Mother
         December 12, 1945 -

Does the caretaker know any of them?
Does he see loving husband at church
or devoted mother buying groceries.
Thinking of them as already under
his care, does he brush off their coats
the way he will one day groom
grass and leaves from their stones?
Do they joke when they see one another?
I'm ready when you are.
                Good to see you here.
Or are they simply names on the wall
that will become names on the ground,
letters and numbers marking a life
that is, that was.

iii.

I'm supposed to collapse
beside the fresh dirt,
wailing over my loss
in uncontrollable grief.
They've marked where
my knees should hit
and where I am to punch
the earth in rage, frustration, and—
the director tells me—
stuff like that.

The irony is
even during the plague years
when I buried a friend
what seemed like every month
and my parents as well,
when I walked around full
of *stuff like that,*
I never wailed
or collapsed,
even into a chair,
but then
I wasn't being filmed.

Now is my chance
to release those emotions
for the money shot,
the scene they'll show
at the Oscars,
but each time the A.D. yells
quiet on the set
I look across
the acres of grass and marble
and giggle.

iv.

If these dead should awaken—
crawl from the earth bewildered,
choking out dirt and grass clods,
relieved,
angry—
what would we say?

Hi.

Welcome back.

How do you feel?

Get out of the shot.

v.

Certain events become markers.
The month my sister married,
the summer my brother spent in Europe,
these were reference points
my family used to orient one another,
but we never mentioned the deaths.
We never used phrases like
that was after grandpa passed away,
which is why I was puzzled,
when sorting my mother's belongings,
by the calendar in her desk.
Dates were circled
with no names or times
or explanations,
and finally I realized
these were the deathdates
of uncles, aunts, parents,
my brother.
My mother had privately recognized
each bitter anniversary,
marking the emptiness
and drawing it into herself.

vi.

Six degrees of separation
must apply to the dead
as well as the living,
and it occurs to me
that I might know someone
buried here
or know someone who knows someone
although I've never heard anyone say,
If you're ever in Parkview,
there's a guy you should look up.

vii.

We shoot the master smoothly,
and the long scenes go okay,
but the simple shots,
the close-ups and cutaways,
cause problems.
Just as the wake, the burial,
the insurance arrangements,
were taken care of
with surprising ease—
others seemed to know
exactly what to do
as if they had rehearsed
the sequence—
and I made quick decisions
about the physical objects,
the office, the clothes, the car,
but I was paralyzed
by the answering machine message,
the magazine subscriptions,
the bills in her name,
the checkup reminder
from the dentist.

viii.

Parkview Memorial, Inc.
issues Walkmans
to the mowing crew
so they can play
the Doors,
Wu-Tang Clan,
Reuben Blades
without disturbing
visitors of the guests.

After all,
just because they work among the dead
it doesn't mean they have to listen to them.

ix.

After each take,
they consult
on whether it was good enough.
Can they use it?
Should they do another?
Perhaps this is what happens
in some Buddhist way;
when the life has been cut,
a decision must be made
to wrap or set up again.

Perhaps our souls are tapes
upon which we repeatedly record
until we get it right,
past lives bleeding through
in ghost images and static.

Or maybe God is only a camera
that we're not to look at directly,
as it impassively records our actions,
the fall of each sparrow,
and each one of us.

x.

This is the glamour of filmmaking,
waiting, trying
not to eat another donut,
wondering when we'll be done,
watching ants crawl
beside a tombstone,
trying to remember
my lines and the reasons
for my lines.

11:00, Friday Night

Standing against the flyer-stapled wall, his beer
on the cigarette machine, his hands hanging
down like delicate white fish, he is ready
to smile if someone should look his way.

While he waits, he makes up stories.
He never writes or tells them. When he tries,
sitting before paper or people, his thoughts
scatter as quick as cockroaches under light.

Visions

I.

Sometimes she feels
herself waiting
for the click, the locking
of the spheres, the snip
across her optic muscle
that will turn her eyes
three degrees and focus in
the happiness that's always
danced at her edges.

She opens herself
once a day, checking her metal
slot where the whistling black man
with a missing finger will push in
the letter, the announcement
that will give her all
the vague things she wants.

She holds herself
rigid, sometimes
thinking a thousand
daily bits of information
have piled until one more
word will fuse and explode
everything she knows
into a searing piece of light.

Her waiting makes her
walk with careful steps
making people admire
the perfect poise
her waiting makes her.

II.

He knows someday he'll drop,
like a handful of hamburger
splattering across patio bricks,
like his father did when his heart
blew through his ribs,
like his grandfather did
from the twelve floor ledge,
like he fantasizes.

He practices sometimes,
going limp. Driving,
pretending it's happened,
his flaccid wrists twist the car
into the waist-high wheat
of a farmer's field until a rut
knocks his foot off the gas
and he must bring himself back
to life and take control.

In the lunchtime crowd, he tries
to will himself black, to crash
his body to the pavement
so when the paramedics
release his hand above his face
it will plummet effortlessly down.

He hopes there won't be any
pain in this silent and cool
absence
of pain he hopes.

Between Diving and Surfacing

Somewhere between diving and surfacing
is that moment
when you're not thinking
about rising or trying
not to rise,
when you're not yet aware
of breathing, of needing
to breathe.

There must be some phrase for this
some other words
maybe in another language
so when they call
and tell me
she's disappeared again
I can say something more
than *maybe*
she's just swimming
underwater.

When My Students Ask Why They Need Poetry

What should I say? Because perhaps they don't.
Now. Or next year. Or ever. These poems won't
get them a job or raise. They may never
feel a connection, need, or desire,
but they may also find in the waiting
room, at the head of the banquet table,
along the road, or by the grave, a poem
will say for them what they cannot. Maybe
they should consider poetry a type
of insurance, like extra batteries,
fire extinguishers, something in case
of emotional emergencies, or
dry socks, a spare key, money stashed away,
a handy resource for what lies ahead.

But even if poems are useful to some,
what of the others? Perhaps it's better
to consider me a kind of merchant
offering poems like bottles of fine wine
so after they have accomplished their goals
of money, fame, and love, and find they have
time for luxuries like literature,
they'll discover, stacked away, a cellar
of ripened poems, waiting to be savored.
What should I say to my students? Maybe
this: Whatever you think of these, take some.
They don't cost you much now and may be worth
a great deal later if you should live long
enough to return to them. I hope you will.

Max

During my office hours
we talk about his grammar
and his bones,
how to anchor a quotation and
how before he had to quit his job
as a mechanic
he could lift a rimmed tire
over his head
with one hand.

One hand
he repeats
raising
an open palm.

But now . . .

> *now . . .*

*they say my spine
is fusing,
and my skeleton is becoming
rigid, brittle,
as fragile as . . .*

> *as . . .*

He searches for the right image,
as precise in his speech
as his writing,
and this concentration,
the way he taps verbs into line,
torquing shut the loose end
of sentences,

suggests how good he must have been
in the shop.
He seems to heft the similes
of eggs and glass
before deciding

. . . as gold to airy thinness beat.

He smiles and gathers
the loose pages
of the day's reading,
photocopied from an anthology
that's now too heavy
for him to carry.

Turning in Grades

Turning in grades
is an act of forgetting.
After the final calculations,
names slide from faces
into files and cabinets,
so that just months later,
when someone calls out,
although you'll recognize
the chin, the eyes, the clothes,
and you may remember
paper topics and titles,
you won't trust yourself
to say a name;
instead you'll smile,
shake hands
ask about coursework,
or vacation or life
after graduation,
all the while wondering
if having taught them
to read closely
and consider not only
what's being said
but what's not
they'll notice
how you treat them
as the most intimate
of strangers.

Sympathy

I often feel bad for sometimes Y,
the afterthought, the part-time vowel,
who never seems to be part of the in-group,
the last pick on the playground,
usually found at the end
of words like the extra person
moving furniture
who places a hand on a corner
in a gesture of helping
or who picks up the little items,
words too small for the other ones
to bother with
by, shy, cry, my
and whose work is threatened by
all those style manuals insisting
we use adverbs sparingly,
cautiously, minimally,
but maybe y
likes it that way
apart, but different,
the clean-up vowel,
an amphibious frog of a letter.

Poetry Lesson

Write a poem
with no people
the teacher says,
Describe the landscape
an animal, the sky,
even a piece of fruit.

Some groan,
some nod,
but no one points out
it's an impossible task.
An apple is an apple
but a poem about an apple
or a dog or the sky,
always has people.
There is always me;
there is always you.

Heaven's Gate

Driving past the guardhouses
which bracket the entrance,
Don explains
no one works in them.
The austere buildings are enough
to keep people out,
and I wonder about Heaven,
the original gated community,
and if St. Peter
has ever patrolled the front,
or if anyone who wants
can simply walk past
the intimidating gates,
the only requirement being
you have to feel
like you belong there.

Last Call

She sings in silent rhythmic tones
I have a heart and it is well
protected by this box
of ribs and more
at each and every tip
a finger with a heart as well.

Joseph Mills holds degrees in literature from the University of Chicago, the University of New Mexico, and the University of California-Davis. He is currently a faculty member at the North Carolina School of the Arts in Winston-Salem, NC, where he teaches English and Humanities. In addition to poetry, Mills writes drama, fiction, non-fiction, and criticism. He authored *Reading Richard Brautigan's Trout Fishing in America*, and co-authored, with his wife Danielle Tarmey, *A Guide to North Carolina's Wineries*. His poetry has appeared in numerous journals and magazines.

Liliana Italiano was born in Buenos Aires, Argentina. She used to dwell in "La Boca" while she was studying at the National Ceramic School, and there she probably inhaled the nostalgic and typically shiny colors one can still enjoy in her latest paintings.

She moved to Cordoba Province and finished her Art studies at the State School of Fine Arts Dr Figueroa Alcorta. She then taught pottery, sculpture and painting at private and public institutions and participated in several exibitions in her home country. Later, she settled in Anizacate, a very small village in the hills where organic shapes and shadow subtleties are at hand. Here she found that her imagination was bound to sensitive observation of ordinary, repetitive things.

In her works, she plays with organic shapes and turns them into a question mark. Nothing is quiet in her work; no absolute affirmatives are allowed. The observer is observed at one and the same time. She wants viewers of her art to explore deeper, get there, and cope with some socio-cultural issues.

Now she lives and works in Charlottesville, Virginia where she has the opportunity to share more widely her sensitive imagination in solo and group exhibitions. Her shows usually include paintings and ceramics. Her work is exhibited in her home country of Argentina, in the USA and across Latin America.

350H23 FM 4077
08/18/09 44400 NC

Printed in the United States
131093LV00001B/107/A

9 780977 228362